K's First Case

L. G. ALEXANDER

Level 3

Series Editors: Andy Hopkins and Jocelyn Potter

Pearson Education Limited

Edinburgh Gate, Harlow,
Essex CM20 2JE, England
and Associated Companies throughout the world.

ISBN: 978-1-4058-8191-3

First published 2000
This edition first published 2008

1 3 5 7 9 10 8 6 4 2

Copyright © Pearson Education Ltd 2008
Illustrations by Gary Wing

Typeset by Graphicraft Ltd, Hong Kong
Set in 11/14pt Bembo
Printed in China
SWTC/01

Published by Pearson Education Ltd in association with
Penguin Books Ltd, both companies being subsidiaries of Pearson Plc

For a complete list of the titles available in the Penguin Readers series please write to your local
Pearson Longman office or to: Penguin Readers Marketing Department, Pearson Education,
Edinburgh Gate, Harlow, Essex CM20 2JE, England.

Contents

Introduction

K, our clever detective, has three important questions:
X murdered Sir Michael Gray, so
1   *How did X murder Sir Michael?*
2   *Who was X?*
3   *Why did X murder Sir Michael?*

Katrina Kirby is a detective, but people call her 'K'. She wants to find the answers to these important questions, but this is her first case. Can you help her?

This is a detective story with a difference. We invite you, the reader, to help K solve the case.

There has been a murder in a big country house in England. One of five people murdered Sir Michael Gray. Sir Michael Gray was in his study at the time of the murder. The study door was locked from the inside. The window was locked from the inside, too, but someone murdered him. Who did it? How? Why?

L.G. Alexander was born in London in 1932. After completing his studies at the University of London in 1954, he became a very successful ELT teacher and writer. His best-known work, *New Concept English* (1967), changed the way that English was taught around the world. This was followed by courses like *Look, Listen and Learn* (1971), *Follow Me* (1980) and *Direct English* (1993–98); practice books like *For and Against* (1968); grammars like the *Longman English Grammar* (1988), and readers like *Dangerous Game* (also a Penguin Reader). All his most important works were published with Longman, part of the Pearson Group.

L.G. Alexander lived with his wife, Julia, in London until his death in 2002.

The people in the story

This is a murder story.

This man was murdered.
His name was Sir Michael Gray.
He was fifty-five years old.
He was very rich.
He was the boss of Cavell and
Company.

Look at this woman.
She is young and pretty and she is
very clever.
She is a detective.
Her name is Katrina Kirby.
People call her 'K'.
She wants to find the answers to some
important questions.
This is her first case.
Can you help her?

K, our clever detective, has three important questions:
X murdered Sir Michael Gray, so
1   How did X murder Sir Michael?
2   Who was X?
3   Why did X murder Sir Michael?

HOW...? WHO...? WHY...?

Who was X?

There was a murder. There were five other people in the house at the time. One of them was X. Who was it?

Lady* Elizabeth Gray,
Sir Michael's wife.
She is forty-eight years old.

Colonel William Fawcett,
Sir Michael's friend.
He is fifty years old.
He was in the army years ago, but he isn't in the army now.

Miss Angela Everett,
Sir Michael's secretary.
She has been Sir Michael's secretary for a year.
She is twenty-five years old.

Andrew Cavell,
Lady Elizabeth's brother.
He is forty years old.
He is one of the bosses of Cavell and Company, too.

Mrs Nancy Flack.
She is the Grays' housekeeper.
She has been with Lady Elizabeth's family for forty years.
She is sixty years old.

*Lord/Lady: title of a man/woman from an upper-class family.

What happened?

The date: November 17th

The time now: 10.15

The place: A large country house in England

November					
1	2	3	4	5	6
7	8	9	10	11	12
13	14	15	16	(17)	18
19	20	21	22	23	24
25	26	27	28	29	30

Sir Michael had dinner with four of the other people at eight o'clock this evening. Then he went to his study. The time was nine o'clock. He locked the door from the inside. He shut the window, too, and locked it from the inside. At 9.30, the housekeeper, Mrs Flack, took some coffee to his room. She knocked at the door. Sir Michael didn't answer. She knocked again and shouted. He didn't answer, so she called three of the other people. They knocked at the door, too, and shouted, but Sir Michael didn't open it. They broke down the study door and went in. They saw Sir Michael's body on the floor. Sir Michael was dead. Lady Elizabeth called the police. The time was 9.40. The police arrived at 9.50 and K arrived with them.

Sir Michael was dead.

3

'We know three things,' the policeman said.

Now it's 10.15 and K is in the study. Sir Michael's dead body isn't here now. The police took photographs of the study and photographs of the body. Then they took the body to the police station. A police doctor has already looked at the body. The police already know the answer to three important questions.

1 Sir Michael didn't die of poison. He drank some whisky at 9.20, but there wasn't any poison in the whisky and there wasn't any poison in Sir Michael's blood.

2 X killed Sir Michael with something sharp through the heart.

3 Sir Michael died at 9.25.

A policeman telephoned K from the police station. 'We know three things,' the policeman said. 'The first thing is: it wasn't poison. The second thing is: it was something sharp – through the heart. The third thing is: Sir Michael died at 9.25.'

The house

Look at this photograph of Sir Michael's house. Its name is 'Flanders'. It's a very big house and it's in a very big garden. There are eight bedrooms upstairs. Downstairs there's an entrance and a kitchen and there are four big rooms: a dining room, a living room, a study and a library.

'Flanders'

Here is a plan of the rooms downstairs. Look at the plan carefully. Sir Michael had dinner with the four other people at eight o'clock this evening. That was in the dining room. Then he went to his study at nine o'clock.

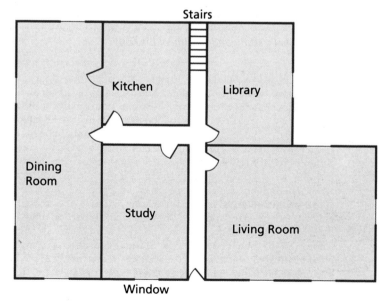

'Flanders': downstairs plan

5

The study and the murder

The murder happened in Sir Michael's study. Here is a police photograph of the study. Look at it carefully and describe it. Then read K's report.

Sir Michael's study and the shape of his body.

Sir Michael's study is large. There is one door into the room. Next to the door there is a fridge. Next to the fridge there is a drinks cupboard. There is a clock on the cupboard. On the wall near the cupboard, there is a picture. On the right there is a window. In the middle of the room there is a big desk. There is a chair behind the desk. There is a bookshelf behind the chair. There are some things on the desk. There is a telephone. Next to the telephone, there is a dictaphone. There are some papers next to the dictaphone. There is a carpet on the floor. Sir Michael's body was on the carpet. The police have drawn the shape of the body on the floor. The feet are near the fridge. There was a whisky glass near Sir Michael's right hand. The glass was empty.

What did K find?

Now look at these pictures carefully and describe them. Then read K's report. K found these things:

Blood and water on Sir Michael's shirt. A hole in the shirt. X killed Sir Michael with something sharp through the heart.

Whisky glass on the floor next to Sir Michael's right hand. A little whisky and water in glass.

Blood and water on the carpet.

Door locked from the inside.

Window locked from the inside.

K didn't find these things:

There wasn't a knife or gun.

Other fingerprints: only Sir Michael's.

There aren't any secret doors or other secret ways into the room.

Sir Michael's body was in front of the fridge. His feet were near the fridge. He was on the carpet, face down. The whisky glass was almost empty. I smelt it. It was in Sir Michael's right hand at the time of the murder. There was blood and water on Sir Michael's shirt – over his heart. Sir Michael was killed with something sharp. There was blood and water on the carpet. X killed Sir Michael with something sharp, so there was blood on Sir Michael's shirt and on the carpet. But why was there water on Sir Michael's shirt and water on the carpet? Sir Michael locked the door from the inside and the window from the inside. There were fingerprints on the desk, on the fridge and on the whisky glass, but they were only Sir Michael's fingerprints. There aren't any secret ways into the room. There wasn't a knife or a gun in the room. Sir Michael's dictaphone was on.

K is writing notes for her report.

Is this what happened?

 9.00 Sir Michael came into the study and locked the door from the inside.

 9.02 He shut the window and locked it from the inside.

 9.05 He sat at his desk and wrote. Then he used the dictaphone.

 9.20 He went to the drinks cupboard. He poured a glass of whisky and drank some.

 9.22 He went to the fridge because he wanted some ice.

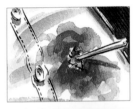

9.25 X came into the room and killed Sir Michael with something sharp. Then X left.

9.30 Mrs Flack knocked at the door and then called three of the other people.

9.35 They broke down the door.

9.40 Lady Elizabeth telephoned the police.

9.50 The police and K arrived.

Is this idea right? If so, then how did X get into the room and how did he or she get out? The window and door were locked from the inside. There aren't any secret doors or other secret ways into the room. Why is there water on Sir Michael's shirt and on the floor?

Other ideas

K's first idea isn't very good. Think of other ideas. Then compare them with K's.

K's second idea

He killed himself. Perhaps he used poison. No. Why? Because there wasn't any poison in the whisky and there wasn't any poison in Sir Michael's blood. Perhaps he used a knife. No. Why? Because there wasn't a knife in the room. So he didn't kill himself.

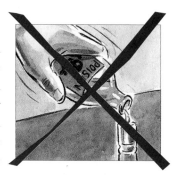

K's third idea

X was already in the room. He or she murdered Sir Michael with a knife and left. X took the knife with him (or her). No. Why? Because the door was locked from the inside and the window was locked from the inside.

K's fourth idea

X used the keyhole. No. Why? The key was in the lock.

Did you think of other ideas?
Did you compare them with K's?
Were they better than hers?

What Sir Michael did every evening (K's report)

Sir Michael arrived home at 7.00 this evening. He arrived with his secretary, Angela Everett. Sir Michael always arrives home at this time, but his secretary doesn't always come with him.

Colonel Fawcett and Andrew Cavell were already at 'Flanders'. They arrived at 5.00 in the afternoon. They had tea with Lady Elizabeth. Mrs Flack brought their tea to the library.

At 7.05 Sir
Michael went
to his room.
He had a bath
and changed for
dinner. He always has
a bath and changes at
this time. Then he
went to the library
and had a drink with
his wife, and with
Colonel Fawcett,
Andrew Cavell and
Angela Everett. Sir
Michael always has a
drink before dinner.

Dinner was
at 8.00. Sir
Michael always
has dinner at
8.00. They all had
dinner in the dining
room. They sat round
the table and talked.

Mrs Flack answers some questions

K sat in Sir Michael's chair in the study and spoke to Mrs Flack.

'So they all had dinner and talked, Mrs Flack?' K asked.

'Yes, miss,' Mrs Flack said.

'Did they laugh, too, Mrs Flack?'

'Oh, yes, miss. They're all good friends.'

'Good friends, Mrs Flack?'

'Yes – well, er – Sir Michael and Lady Elizabeth, well – they often . . .'

'They often had disagreements, Mrs Flack?'

'Yes, miss, but not this evening at dinner. After dinner Sir Michael and Lady Elizabeth went to the library. Just the two of them. I knew they were fighting. I could hear them. I was in the kitchen. They shouted and shouted. We all heard them.'

'Then what?'

'Then Sir Michael went to his study.'

'What time was that?'

'It was nine o'clock.'

'Did Sir Michael always go to his study at nine o'clock?'

'Yes, always, miss. He worked in his study from 9.00 until 1.00 or 2.00 in the morning. Sometimes his secretary went to his study with him,' Mrs Flack said.

Mrs Flack answers some questions.

'Sometimes? Did she go there this evening?'

'No, miss. I took Sir Michael a cup of coffee at 9.30. I always take him a cup of coffee at 9.30. I knocked at the study door but

14

'We found him on the floor.'

he didn't answer. I knocked again and again. I shouted but he didn't answer. So I called Lady Elizabeth, Colonel Fawcett and Mr Cavell.'

'And Miss Everett?'

'No, miss. She was in the garden. Colonel Fawcett and Mr Cavell broke down the door and we found him – Sir Michael – we found him on the floor – dead! Oh, miss!' Mrs Flack cried. She was very sad.

'Thank you, Mrs Flack,' K said quietly.

Lady Elizabeth's story

Mrs Flack left the study and K wrote her report. Then there was a knock at the door. It was very quiet.

'Come in,' K said softly. The door opened.

'You wanted to see me,' Lady Elizabeth said.

'Yes, Lady Elizabeth. Come in and sit down, please. Would you like a drink?'

'No, thank you, Inspector.'

'How are you?' K asked quietly.

'How can you ask? Mike's gone. He's dead. Dead! It isn't true, is it, Inspector? It can't be true!'

'Sshh!' K said. 'Tell me about him.'

'Mike? He was a good husband. We married twenty-five years ago. That's a long time, isn't it? He was just out of the army then. He loved me and I loved him. We didn't have any children and Mike was sorry about that. But he was always a good husband to me.'

'You wanted to see me,'
Lady Elizabeth said.

'Always?'

'Yes, always!' Lady Elizabeth shouted. 'Well – there were . . .'

'Yes?' K asked quietly.

'Other women. All these secretaries!' Lady Elizabeth cried. 'Mike liked young secretaries – and they liked him. For his money! Look at this new one. This . . . this . . . What's her name? This Angela Everett. The little . . . !' Lady Elizabeth's voice was quiet but her face was red and her eyes were angry.

16

'Oh,' she continued, 'I hated Mike's secretaries. They were always young, always pretty and they took him away from me. But I *really* hate this secretary. This Angela Everett. She comes into my house every day. She comes with Mike. "I'm sorry, Lady Elizabeth," she says in her pretty little voice. "I must take Sir Michael from you. We have work to do." Mike loved me. I know it! I know it! But he liked other women. He was rich, so women liked him. Yes, I loved Mike, but sometimes I hated him. I hated him! Perhaps he's in this room now. Perhaps he can hear me. I loved him and I hated him. He knew that well.'

'What happened this evening?' K asked.

'I'll tell you,' Lady Elizabeth said.

'I loved him and I hated him.'

After dinner...

18

'So Sir Michael went to his study at nine o'clock. What did *you* do?' K asked.

'I went to the living room because I wanted to speak to my brother, Andrew. We sat and talked. I told him about Mike and about that woman, Everett. Andrew knows all about it.'

'Sir Michael was in the study. Did you hear him?'

'No. At 9.30 I heard Nancy shouting. Andrew and I ran to the study. The door was locked. Andrew and Colonel Fawcett broke down the door. Then I saw Mike's body on the floor. He was dead! I telephoned the police.'

'Where was Miss Everett?' K asked.

'In the garden. She often went to the study after dinner.'

'But not tonight?'

'No. Not tonight. She was in the garden. Why did Mike die? He didn't kill himself, so perhaps she knows. Perhaps she can tell you. A woman like that can't bring good to this house. Can I go now?' Lady Elizabeth asked suddenly.

'Of course,' K said. 'Thank you, Lady Elizabeth.'

'Can I go now?' Lady Elizabeth asked suddenly.

Colonel Fawcett's story

The time was 10.45. There was a knock at the study door.

'Can I come in?' a voice asked. It was a man's voice.

'Yes,' K said.

The door opened and Colonel Fawcett came in. 'You want to see all of us tonight, Inspector?'

'Yes,' K said. 'A drink, Colonel Fawcett?'

'Yes, please.'

'Shall I get you a whisky?'

'Yes, please. I need one!'

'Would you like some ice?'

'Ice? Er – er – no, thank you. I don't want any ice. Just water, please. Thank you.'

'He was your friend,' K said.

'Yes. A very good friend, too,' the Colonel said, putting his head between his hands. 'Dead! Michael Gray dead! I can't believe it.'

'It's sad,' K said, 'but it's true. Tell me about him.'

'We were in the army together. That was twenty-five years ago. Then Michael left the army, married Elizabeth and went into Cavell and Company. That's Lady Elizabeth's family business. She was a Cavell. I left the army five years ago. I'm not in the army

'Dead! Michael Gray dead! I can't believe it!'

20

now but people still call me "Colonel". I needed work so I went to my old friend, Michael. He helped me.'

'Helped you? How?' K asked.

'Oh – er – um. Money. You know.'

'I don't know,' K said.

'He gave me money.'

'*Gave* you?'

'Lent me.'

'How much did he lend you?'

'Well – £50,000.'

'Mm. And what did you do with it?'

'I put it into my business.'

'What *is* your business, Colonel Fawcett?'

'Well, it isn't really a *business* . . . horses . . . you know.'

'You gambled the money,' K said.

'Yes, I gambled and lost,' the Colonel said. 'Michael knew about this. He was very angry with me. He said, "I lent you this money and now you must pay it back to me." I said, "I can't. I haven't any money!" He said, "Then you must sell your house!" I didn't want to sell my house. We couldn't agree about that.'

'He's dead now,' K said. 'Are you really sorry?'

'Sorry? Of course I'm sorry. We couldn't agree about money, but we were friends. Good friends. Army friends are always good friends.'

'What did you do in the army, Colonel?'

'I was with the engineers. Michael was with the engineers, too.'

'Are you an engineer?'

'I *was* an engineer.'

'And now you gamble with other people's money,' K said.

'I gambled and lost.'

'So you had a fight with Sir Michael about money. Tell me about it.'

'Tell me about tonight.'

'Tonight? After dinner I went to the living room. I went with Andrew. Michael and Elizabeth went to the library. They were fighting. We heard them from the living room. They often had fights, Michael and Elizabeth. Michael – you know – he liked women. And Angela, well, she's a pretty little thing.' The Colonel smiled. 'Just like you, Inspector. A pretty little thing.'

'Thank you, Colonel,' K said coldly and smiled. 'What did you do after dinner?'

'Well, Michael went to his study. Elizabeth came to the living room and I went to the library. I sat in the library and read.'

'Alone?'

'Yes, alone. The housekeeper, Mrs Flack, brought me some coffee at 9.30. Then she took some coffee to Michael. His door was locked. Then I heard her shouting. I ran to the study. You know the story.'

'Yes, but not all the story – yet!' K said. 'You can go now, Colonel, and please call Miss Everett for me.'

'Just like you, Inspector. A pretty little thing.'

Angela Everett's story

'I don't like this room,' Miss Everett said as she came in. 'Mick died in here. Only two hours ago – Mick died in here. Why do you use this room?'

'I have my reasons,' K said. 'Sit down, Miss Everett. Can I offer you a drink?'

'Yes, please. I'd like a very large whisky and a lot of ice, please.'

K went to the fridge.

*'Colonel Fawcett calls you
"a pretty little thing".'*

She opened it, then she opened the freezer and took out the ice-tray. She put some ice in Miss Everett's drink and then put the ice-tray back in the freezer. K looked into the freezer, then she looked at Miss Everett.

'Why are you looking at me like that?' Miss Everett asked suddenly.

'Colonel Fawcett calls you "a pretty little thing". Are you?' K asked.

'Are *you*?' Miss Everett asked. She spoke coldly, too.

'*I'm* asking the questions,' K answered. 'Here's your drink.'

'Thanks.'

'Sir Michael loved you.'

'Of course he did. Didn't *she* tell you?'

'*She*?'

'That woman. His wife. *She* didn't love him. She had fights with him. All the time. She had fights with my Mick.'

24

'Mick?'

'Yes, he was "Mick" to me. "Mike" to her. "Michael" to other people. My Mick loved me. She always shouted at him. So he came to me. *She* gave him hate. I gave him love.'

'You really loved him?'

'Of course. I loved him deeply. And she knew it. I hate her. I hate that woman,' Miss Everett shouted. 'She hated my Mick. That's why I hate her. She murdered him. I know it. I know it.'

'Sir Michael was fifty-five. And you are twenty-five.'

'What are you suggesting?' Miss Everett asked. 'Don't you know any nice men of fifty-five? Mick was nice. Really nice.'

'And rich,' K said. 'He left a lot of money to you, in his will.'

'And rich,' K said.

25

'Really? How do you know that?'

'I'm asking the questions. You're here to answer them,' K said. 'Didn't you know about the money?'

'Yes,' Miss Everett answered.

'How much did he leave you?'

'I don't know.'

'You know very well. Tell me,' K said.

'Mick changed his will two weeks ago. He left a lot of money to *her*, of course. She doesn't need money. She's rich. But he left £100,000 to me. He told me about it.'

'Sir Michael's death is a good thing for you, isn't it?'

'Good for me? What are you suggesting? I loved him. Don't you understand?'

'Oh, I understand, but perhaps you're rich now. Perhaps you have £100,000.'

'Are you jealous?' Miss Everett asked K. 'Listen, policewoman, I love money. That's true. But I loved Mick. Do you hear? I loved

'Listen, policewoman, I love money.'

Mick. Why did the police send a *woman* detective?' Miss Everett asked.

'Why don't you ask them?' K answered.

'You're pretty,' Miss Everett said. 'My Mick liked pretty women. His wife was a pretty woman years ago, but she isn't now.'

'I must tell her that,' K said.

'Yes. Tell her. Please tell her I said so!'

'You often went to the study with Sir Michael after dinner.'

'Yes. We worked together. We usually went to the study at 9.00. I had a whisky with Mick. Then we worked. The housekeeper usually brought us a cup of coffee at 9.30. I worked until 11.00, then I went home.'

'But you didn't go to Sir Michael's study tonight?'

'No, I didn't. It's strange.'

'Strange?'

'Yes, Mick didn't want me to go. He wanted to be alone.'

'Tell me about it.'

'He wanted to be alone.'

'And where were you tonight – at the time of the murder?'

'In the garden.'

'Where, in the garden?'

'Outside Mick's study.'

'Why?'

'I wanted to walk. It's a cold night but it's fine. I needed air. Mick was in his study. I wanted to be with him and I was alone. I didn't want to stay in the house.'

'You were afraid,' K said.

'Afraid? Why?'

'Perhaps Sir Michael wanted to change his will again. You were afraid of that. You didn't want that, did you?'

'That's not true. I only wanted to be with him. It wasn't the money.'

'You want to be a rich woman.'

'Quiet!' Miss Everett shouted. 'I'm pretty and you hate me. You like *her*. Well, listen. I didn't do it. I didn't do it!' Miss Everett ran out of the room.

Miss Everett ran out of the room.

Andrew Cavell's story

'Can I come in?' a voice said. The voice was calm, cold, upper-class.

'Yes, and shut the door please,' K said. She looked up.

'It's me. Andrew Cavell. Miss Everett has left – I think.'

K looked at this proud man in his fine suit.

'Miss Everett has left – you think,' K said.

'I heard her. We all heard her,' Mr Cavell laughed.

'A little whisky, Mr Cavell?' K asked.

'Yes, please.'

'Shall I get you some ice?'

'Er – no, thanks. Just water, please. Thank you.'

'What can you tell me about Sir Michael?'

'A lot. What do you want to know?'

'A lot.'

'Well, I didn't like him. I can tell you that. He was my sister's husband, but I didn't like Michael Gray at all. I never liked him.

K looked at this proud man in his fine suit.

30

'Michael Gray married my sister twenty-five years ago. He wasn't a rich man then – just out of the army. We – the family – took him into the company. My father, Lord Cavell, liked him. He worked hard and before long he became the boss of Cavell and Company. Cavell and Company is the family business. Michael was a hard worker, but he married into money.'

'You never liked him. Why?'

'For a number of reasons. He often had fights with Elizabeth and I didn't like that at all. He liked women and he spent a lot of money on them. But he spent money like water. I didn't like that. It's our money, the family's. He changed his will. My sister told me about it. He wanted to leave £100,000 to that silly girl, Angela Everett.'

'His secretary.'

'Yes – his secretary.'

'Why did you come to "Flanders", Mr Cavell?'

'I wanted to speak to Michael. We had a talk before dinner.'

'Tell me about it.'

'We had a talk before dinner.'

31

'Well, he's dead now, so that's good for Cavell and Company.'

'Yes, it's excellent.'

'And you're glad?'

'Yes. He's dead and I'm glad. The family business is more important to me than Michael Gray. Of course, I'm sorry for my sister. She really loved him.'

'*Did* Sir Michael leave £100,000 to Miss Everett?'

'I don't know. I haven't seen the will. He talked about it.'

'Perhaps Miss Everett is a rich woman now.'

'Perhaps she is.'

'You're a cold man, Mr Cavell.'

'Cold?'

'Yes. He's dead and you're glad. Perhaps he *has* left £100,000 to his secretary, but you don't even look angry. You really hated Sir Michael, didn't you? Behind that calm face, you hated him.'

'Behind that calm face, you hated him.'

'True, madam, but I didn't murder him.'

'Sir Michael died at 9.25. Where were you at the time?'

'Hasn't my sister told you? I was in the living room. She spoke to me about Everett. Then we heard Nancy – Mrs Flack. We ran outside. We ran to the study door. Colonel Fawcett and I broke down the door. We saw the body on the floor – just there. Elizabeth immediately telephoned the police.'

'Did you touch the body?'

'No. Michael was dead. We all saw that and we didn't touch the body. We just waited for the police.'

'And the police sent *me*.'

'Yes, madam. The police sent *you*.'

'Thank you, Mr Cavell.'

'Excuse me, but can we all go to bed now?'

'No, I'm sorry. It's late, but I must speak to all of you. But first I must speak to Mrs Flack again.'

'I'll send her to you.'

'Thank you, Mr Cavell.'

'Yes, madam. The police sent you.'

Nancy Flack's story

'Whisky, Mrs Flack?'

    'Oh, yes, please, miss. I'd like a large one.'

'You like whisky, Mrs Flack?'

    'Er . . . well, miss . . . I . . .'

'You often drink Sir Michael's whisky . . . ?'

    'I . . . well . . . I . . .'

'Ice?'

    'No, no, thank you. Well, yes, please.'

    K took the ice-tray out of the freezer. She took a piece of ice out of it and put it in the whisky. 'Look at this tray, Mrs Flack.'

'Look at this tray, Mrs Flack.'

'I love my Lady Elizabeth.'

'What about it, miss? I filled it this morning.'

'Well, Sir Michael died here – in front of the fridge. He had a glass of whisky in his hand. He wanted some ice, so he went to the fridge. He didn't get any ice.'

'How do you know, miss?'

'Only you and Miss Everett have had ice in your whisky. That's two pieces. Sir Michael didn't have any. That's strange, isn't it?'

'Yes, miss, it's very strange.'

'How long have you been with the family?'

'Forty years.'

'That's a long time.'

'Yes, miss. Lady Elizabeth was a little girl then – eight years old. Mr Andrew was a baby. I worked for Lord and Lady Cavell. They're dead now.'

'You like the family?'

'Yes, miss. I love them all. They're all very kind to me. I love my Lady Elizabeth.'

'And Sir Michael? Did you love him?'

'Yes, miss. I loved him, too. They married twenty-five years ago. I remember it well. I've worked for them since then. Sir Michael was a good man. A kind man.'

'He and Lady Elizabeth often had fights.'

'Yes, miss. But he loved her deeply and she loved him.'

'But he liked pretty girls.'

'He was a man, miss.'

'And Miss Everett? What about her?'

'Oh, I don't like her, miss. I was always afraid of her.'

'Afraid?'

'Yes, miss. She wasn't like the other girls. Sir Michael listened to her. "Perhaps they'll run away and leave Lady Elizabeth," I thought, and I didn't like that.'

'You were afraid of it.'

'Yes.'

'Why?'

'Well . . . I clean this study every day, miss and . . .'

'And you always read Sir Michael's letters?'

'I . . . er . . . yes, miss.'

'Tell me about it.'

'And you always read Sir Michael's letters?'

It was last week when I was cleaning the study.

This desk! Oh! What's this? Mm. A letter. Her writing. I must read it.

'My dearest Mick –' The little . . . !

My dearest Mick,
I love you my dearest Mick
I want to be with you.
Can't we be together always.
Can't we? You can leave
that woman and we can
live together. We can have
such good times when
. . . in the
. . . the

Suddenly the door opened and Sir Michael came in.

What are you doing, Nancy?

Er . . . er . . . just cleaning the study, sir.

I put the letter in my pocket.

I left the study and took it with me.

I read it in my room, then I put it back on Sir Michael's desk . . .

. . . I was afraid.

'Now they can't run away together. Aren't you glad, Mrs Flack?'

'No, miss.'

'No?'

'No, because Sir Michael's dead. I didn't want Sir Michael to run away with Miss Everett. But I didn't want him to die. I looked after him for twenty-five years, miss.'

'You're very loyal to this family, Mrs Flack.'

'Yes, miss. That's the word, "loyal". I don't know why. You see, I haven't got a family, miss. *This* is my family. Now I want to be with Lady Elizabeth. Always. I want to help her and look after her. Miss Everett is a bad woman. Sir Michael is dead. She's taken Sir Michael from us. She's really bad, miss.'

'Tell me about tonight, Mrs Flack.'

'She's really bad, miss.'

'Well, miss. Dinner was at 8.00. After dinner I made some coffee for Colonel Fawcett and some coffee for Sir Michael. I always take – er – took – coffee to Sir Michael after dinner. Lady Elizabeth and Mr Andrew were in the living room. They didn't want any coffee. I took the coffee to Colonel Fawcett in the library. Then I went to the study with Sir Michael's coffee. I knocked at the door but he didn't answer. I tried to open the door, but it was locked – you know the story, miss.'

'Yes. You shouted and three of the others came. Miss Everett didn't come.'

'No, miss. She says she was in the garden.'

'She *was* in the garden, Mrs Flack. Then Colonel Fawcett and Mr Andrew broke down the door. And you saw Sir Michael. He was right there,' K said, pointing, 'right there, just behind you. On the floor. Dead!'

Mrs Flack looked behind her and jumped. 'Yes, miss. Just there!' She put her head between her hands and cried.

'You can go now, Mrs Flack. Thank you.'

Mrs Flack looked behind her and jumped.

40

Who did it? You decide!

1   Lady Elizabeth murdered her husband because:
    a) she was jealous of Angela Everett. ☐
    b) she hated him. ☐
    c) her brother wanted it. ☐

2   Colonel Fawcett murdered Sir Michael because:
    a) he was afraid of him. ☐
    b) he didn't want to pay back the £50,000. ☐
    c) he gambled. ☐

3   Angela Everett murdered Sir Michael because:
    a) she was jealous of Lady Gray. ☐
    b) she wanted £100,000. ☐
    c) she hated him. ☐

4 Andrew Cavell murdered
   Sir Michael because:
   a) he didn't like him. ☐
   b) he wanted to save his
      company. ☐
   c) he wanted to save
      his sister. ☐

5 Nancy Flack murdered
   Sir Michael because:
   a) she always read his letters. ☐
   b) she drank a lot. ☐
   c) she didn't want him to
      run away with Angela
      Everett. ☐

Who do you choose? X is:
   a) Lady Elizabeth. ☐
   b) Colonel Fawcett. ☐
   c) Angela Everett. ☐
   d) Andrew Cavell. ☐
   e) Nancy Flack. ☐

K's notes

All these people had a reason to kill Sir Michael.

Lady Elizabeth

Reason: Jealousy

Notes: Lady Gray really loved her husband and he loved her. But he liked women and Lady Gray was very jealous. She was jealous of all Sir Michael's secretaries, but she was <u>very</u> jealous of Angela Everett. She wanted to punish her husband, so she murdered him.

Colonel Fawcett

Reason: Money

Notes: Sir Michael really wanted his money back and Colonel Fawcett didn't want to pay it. He didn't want to sell his house. He gambled and lost the money in a silly way. He was afraid, so he murdered Sir Michael.

Angela Everett

Reason: Money

Notes: She didn't love Sir Michael and he didn't love her. She only wanted his money. Did Sir Michael leave money to her in his new will? Yes, Angela thought. She wanted £100,000, so she murdered Sir Michael.

Andrew Cavell

Reason: Loyal to his family and to the business, Cavell and Company.

Notes: He's a cold man. He really didn't like Sir Michael. Sir Michael 'spent money like water' and he was worried about this. He wanted to save the company, so he murdered Sir Michael.

Nancy Flack

Reason: Loyal to Lady Elizabeth

Notes: She has looked after the Cavells and the Grays for 40 years. She really loves Lady Gray and she loved Sir Michael, but she hated Angela Everett. This question worried her: Is Sir Michael going to run away with Everett? She wanted to stop this and to punish Sir Michael. So she murdered him.

1.30: In the study

'It's very late. I know and I'm sorry. I'm sorry for all this trouble. You're all tired. Please sit down. Mrs Flack has brought us some coffee. That's very kind, Mrs Flack. Thank you. It's late and we all want to go to bed, but I must speak to you. Of course, I've spoken to you alone, one by one. There are three questions which I must answer:

1 Who murdered Sir Michael? One of you murdered him. You are sitting there. You are looking at me and there is murder in your heart. Perhaps I know your name, perhaps I don't. I can't tell you yet.

2 Why did X murder Sir Michael? You all have reasons. Perhaps you were jealous, perhaps you wanted money, perhaps you were loyal. I can't answer this question yet.

3 How did X murder Sir Michael? Don't tell me. I can save you the trouble. I know the answer to this question now. I can tell you.'

'I know the answer to this question.'

44

What happened between 9.00 and 9.25?

'Sir Michael's death was strange. He was alone in the room, and the door and window were locked from the inside. X didn't come into the room and didn't leave the room at the time of the murder. X prepared the murder carefully. How did X prepare the murder? I know the answer – I think. You all know very well what Sir Michael did every day. Sir Michael always went to his study after dinner. Sometimes his secretary went with him, but she didn't go with him tonight. Sir Michael always had a drink and worked until late. Mrs Flack always brought him some coffee after dinner. What happened between 9.00 and 9.25? That's the question. I won't answer it yet. I want to say one thing. Sir Michael was 180 centimetres tall. Now look at the fridge. The freezer is 143 centimetres above the floor. This is important. The freezer is in line with Sir Michael's heart. What happened?'

Try to answer K's question –

DON'T TURN OVER YET!

'The freezer is in line with Sir Michael's heart.'

'Sir Michael went into his study at 9.00. He locked the door and the window. Then at 9.02 he sat down at his desk and wrote. Then from 9.15 until 9.20 he used the dictaphone. At 9.20 he went to the drinks cupboard. He wanted some whisky. He poured some whisky into a glass and then a little water. He drank some. Then he wanted some ice. After opening the fridge, he opened the freezer. He pulled the ice-tray with his left hand and then what happened? He started a mechanism which was in line with his heart. This mechanism shot an icicle into Sir Michael's heart. Sir Michael turned and fell to the floor. He was dead. The glass fell out of his right hand. The icicle was in his heart, so there was blood and water on his shirt and blood and water on the carpet. There wasn't a gun or a knife. The sharp "knife" was an icicle. It disappeared – and there was only water!

'The mechanism is still in the wall behind the freezer. It isn't working now. One of you put it there. One of you came into this room before Sir Michael and put it there. Who was it?' K asked. 'I want to know.

'Was it you, Lady Elizabeth?' K asked. 'You were jealous of Sir Michael's secretaries. You hate Angela Everett and you wanted to punish your husband.'

'This mechanism shot an icicle into
Sir Michael's heart.'

'No, no. I didn't do it. I loved him. I loved him.'

'Was it you, Colonel Fawcett? He lent you a lot of money. You gambled it on horses and lost it. He wanted it back.'

'Of course not, Inspector. He was my friend.'

'And you, Miss Everett? He changed his will and perhaps he left you £100,000. That's a lot of money and just what you wanted.'

'I did it. You think that, don't you, policewoman? Well I didn't!' Angela Everett shouted the words at K.

'And you, Mr Cavell, always so calm? You were worried about the £100,000. You wanted to save the company. Sir Michael spent money on women and you didn't like it.'

Mr Cavell didn't answer.

'And you, Mrs Flack? You read his letters. You wanted to punish him.'

'Oh, miss, I didn't, miss, really I didn't. I didn't do it.'

'Between 9.02 and 9.25 Sir Michael wrote at his desk. What did he write? That's the question. He wrote a letter to Andrew Cavell. I have it here. I'll read some of it to you. *Dear Andrew, You're worried about money, I know. I changed my will two weeks ago, but I didn't leave any money to Angela. She thinks so, but I didn't. She's a silly girl and I'm tired of her. Perhaps I need a new secretary...*'

'Oh!' Angela cried. 'The pig! The pig!' She shouted the word 'pig'.

'And at 9.15 he used his dictaphone. What did he say? Listen to his voice... "Angela, my dearest. You're a nice girl and you've been good to me, but it can't continue. I'm speaking these words to you because I don't want to write a letter. I want to speak to you. I want to say goodbye to you. You're a young woman and your life is in front of you. Goodbye, my dearest. I only..."'

'Why? Why?' Angela screamed. 'The pig! I hate him. I hate all of you! I hate you! I hate you!'

'You took him from me!' Lady Elizabeth cried.

'Quiet!' Miss Everett shouted. 'You can have him. He's dead! You and your family! You Grays and Cavells. All so upper-class! With your fine houses and your fine cars and your money! You can only think of money. He never loved me and I knew it. An old man of fifty-five! Pah! And I didn't love him. Yes, I wanted his money, but I couldn't have it. Of course I didn't murder him. One of *you* did that. Thanks. You saved me the trouble. He's dead and I'm glad.'

Putting her face in her hands, Miss Everett ran out of the room. There were tears in her eyes.

Colonel Fawcett got up. 'No, don't follow her, Colonel Fawcett,' K said. 'She won't leave. She can't leave. My people are all round the house.'

'She called Sir Michael a pig!' Mrs Flack cried. 'Did you hear, miss? That woman called Sir Michael a pig!'

'No, don't follow her, Colonel Fawcett.'

Goodnight

K looked at her watch. It was 2.25. 'We must all go to bed,' she said. 'We're all tired.' Then she spoke to Lady Elizabeth. 'It's very late, Lady Elizabeth,' K said, 'and I can't leave this house. You must all stay in the house, too. You can't leave, so don't try. There are police all round it. Where can I sleep, Lady Elizabeth?' K asked. 'I don't want to stay in this room.'

'There's a room upstairs,' Lady Elizabeth said. 'You can sleep there, Inspector.'

'Thank you, Lady Elizabeth. Goodnight to you all,' K said.

'Goodnight, Inspector,' they all said.

They all left the study and went upstairs to their bedrooms. Kay went upstairs, too.

They went upstairs to their bedrooms.

A shape in the dark

It was three o'clock in the morning. It was very dark and the house was very quiet. K went downstairs quietly and went back to the study. She sat in Sir Michael's chair and waited...3.15...3.30...3.45...4.00...4.15...4.30...K was very tired. She only wanted to sleep...to sleep...to sleep.

Suddenly she looked up! She heard a noise. It was the study door. The door opened very quietly. K saw a shape in the dark. She saw the shape of a man! K could see very well in the dark. She watched and listened. The person went to the fridge. He pulled the fridge quietly from the wall. Then he pulled a small box out of the wall. 'The mechanism! He's come for the mechanism!' K thought. She got up and went quietly towards the dark shape. The man looked at the box and didn't hear K.

'Don't move!' K said softly. 'Don't move, or...'

'Aaah...!' the man cried. He tried to run out of the room.

DON'T TURN OVER YET!

Who is the man in the dark? You decide!

Colonel Fawcett

Andrew Cavell

K jumped on the man and held his arms. She hit the man hard in the neck. Then a quick move and he was on the floor!

'Aargh!' the man cried. Suddenly K turned on the light and looked down at the floor.

'Colonel Fawcett!' she cried.

'Yes, Inspector. It's me. Ooh! Please don't hit me again. You're a pretty little thing, but you fight like a man. Ooh!' Colonel Fawcett touched his neck lightly.

'You came for the mechanism,' K said. 'I waited for you. I've been here since three o'clock. I was sleepy five minutes ago, but I'm not sleepy now!'

The mechanism was on the floor. Colonel Fawcett took it in his right hand. 'I didn't think . . .' he said. 'I didn't think . . .' and his voice died away.

'Colonel Fawcett!' she cried.

The answer to K's first question: How...?

'Just a minute, Inspector,' Colonel Fawcett said suddenly. 'I'm not the murderer. You don't think that, do you?'

'Then why are you here?' K asked.

'I wanted to see this mechanism. I'm an engineer, remember? I tried to sleep, but I couldn't. I thought about this mechanism. How clever, I thought, I must see it. So I came downstairs. After moving the fridge, I got the mechanism out of the wall. Then you attacked me. Ooh! You really hurt me.' Colonel Fawcett touched his neck again. 'But look at this mechanism! You see? It was behind the fridge. The box went into the wall and this piece went into the back of the freezer. This string was tied to the ice-tray. Michael pulled the ice-tray and this worked the mechanism. It was in line with his heart. Look inside the box. See? It's a strong bow. Very small, of course. And it shoots icicles! Michael opened the freezer, pulled the ice-tray and WHAM! – an icicle through the heart! Then it turned to water and disappeared. The "knife" just disappeared! Very clever!'

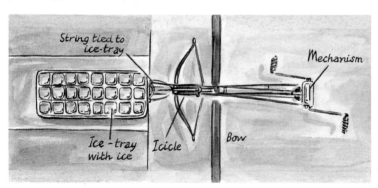

The mechanism

'Michael made this bow,' Colonel Fawcett said. 'It's small but strong. The murderer put an icicle in the freezer just before nine o'clock. Michael pulled the ice-tray. It was frozen to the bottom of the freezer. So he pulled it hard. The icicle went into the string on the bow. The string went back and WHAM! Michael was shot through the heart. Very clever!'

'Sir Michael made this bow?' K asked.

'Yes. He often made things like this in the army.' Suddenly Colonel Fawcett stopped. He spoke slowly. 'Michael made this bow and it killed him. Who put it behind the fridge? Not me!'

'You didn't. I know,' K said.

'Then who . . . ?'

'I'll answer that question *now*!' K said softly. 'Sshh!' She walked to the door very quietly. Then she suddenly opened the door.

'Aaaah!'

There's a person outside the door. Who is it? You decide!

Lady Elizabeth

Miss Everett

Andrew Cavell

Nancy Flack

The answer to K's second question: Who . . . ?

'Nancy!' K cried.

'Oh, miss!' Mrs Flack cried.

'Nancy!' K said. 'What are you doing there?'

Mrs Flack didn't answer.

'You're listening, aren't you, Nancy?'

'Yes, miss,' Mrs Flack said.

K pulled Nancy into the room. 'Now answer me. Why are you listening?'

'I want to know. . . I want to know. . . about the murder, miss.'

'Yes. You want to know,' K said. 'This bow was in the wall behind the fridge. You wanted to take it out. And why did you want to take it out?'

Mrs Flack didn't answer.

'You can't answer? Then I'll tell you. You wanted to take it out because you put it there. You put it there before nine o'clock last night.'

Mrs Flack still didn't answer.

'Didn't you?' K shouted.

'Yes, miss,' Mrs Flack said softly.

The lights went on all over the house. First Angela Everett came downstairs, then Andrew Cavell, then Lady Elizabeth. They all went into the study.

'Oh, I'm so sleepy,' Miss Everett said. 'What's happening? What's all this noise?'

'Oh, miss!' Mrs Flack cried.

55

Andrew Cavell looked at the bow and then at Mrs Flack. But he didn't speak. Lady Elizabeth looked at the bow and then at Mrs Flack. 'That's Michael's,' she said. 'He made it. He often made things like that.' She went to Mrs Flack and held her arms. 'Now look at me, Nancy,' she said quietly. 'Look into my eyes.' Mrs Flack looked up slowly. 'Look into my eyes,' Lady Elizabeth repeated. Mrs Flack looked into Lady Elizabeth's eyes. 'Now tell me. You didn't do it. Tell me that please, Nancy. You didn't kill my husband.'

'But I did, my Lady,' Mrs Flack said. 'I killed him, but . . .'

'Nancy!' Lady Elizabeth screamed. 'Oh, Nancy! How could you, Nancy? How could you? You've looked after my family for forty years, Nancy. You came to this family forty years ago. I was a

'Look into my eyes.'

56

child of eight. Andrew was a baby. You love us. We love you. You've looked after Michael for twenty-five years. You loved him, too. Nancy, you couldn't do this bad thing. You couldn't! You couldn't! Why, Nancy, why?'

'Oh, my Lady,' Nancy said with tears in her eyes. 'Sir Michael made this bow. I took it and made a plan. I came into this study last night at 8.50. You didn't hear me. I put an icicle in the freezer. I made the icicle in the big fridge in the kitchen. I put the mechanism in the wall behind the freezer a week ago. I prepared the mechanism a month ago. Last night I put the icicle into place. Last night was the night. I worked carefully and didn't leave any fingerprints. I've prepared for a long time for last night.'

'Yes, but why did you do it?' Lady Elizabeth said.

'Oh, my Lady,' Nancy said with tears in her eyes.

The answer to K's third question: Why...?

'But, my Lady, I didn't want to kill Sir Michael. I loved him and I love you. He wasn't always kind to you and you often had fights. He went with other women. But I wanted to kill that woman there! That bad woman, Everett. She usually came to the study with Sir Michael. She did the same thing every day. She poured some whisky into a glass for Sir Michael. She put some ice in the whisky. I prepared this mechanism very carefully for her, but last night she didn't come. She was in the garden. I didn't know that at the time. I was in the kitchen. At 9.30 I brought the coffee and Sir Michael didn't open the door. Then I knew. He was dead! Dead! And that woman, that bad woman wasn't! Oh, my Lady, what could I do? What could I do?' Tears ran down Mrs Flack's face.

A policewoman went to her and said softly, 'Come to the station with us now, Mrs Flack.' She took Mrs Flack out of the room.

'What could I do? What could I do?' Mrs Flack said again and again.

'I wanted to kill that woman there!'

Goodbye

It's early morning. The sun is just coming up in the cold blue sky. A pretty girl is sitting in a fast car. She looks happy. The fast car is just outside 'Flanders'. Three people are standing next to the car: Lady Elizabeth, Andrew Cavell and Colonel Fawcett. They say goodbye. The pretty girl speaks to Colonel Fawcett. 'Where's Miss Everett?'

'She's already gone,' the Colonel said. 'I called you "a pretty little thing" – and you are!' Colonel Fawcett laughed.

'Thank you, Colonel. I'm not working now. I've changed my clothes. That's the end of my first case. I'm not "K" now. I'm Katrina Kirby. The day's just starting. Goodbye!'

'Goodbye!' the Colonel called.

Brrm! The sound of the big car broke the quiet of the morning. Brrm! Brrm! The fast car disappeared into the early morning sun.

'I'm not working now.'

ACTIVITIES

Pages 1–8

Before you read

1 This story is called *K's First Case*. Discuss these questions.

    a Find this meaning of the word *case* in the Word List at the back of the book. What kind of story is this?

    b How do you think 'K' feels?

2 Read the Introduction to the book and answer the questions.

    a Who has died in this story?

    b Where did he die?

    c Why does Katrina Kirby have questions?

While you read

3 Is this information about the case right (✓), wrong (✗) or don't we know (?)?

    a Sir Michael worked with his brother. .....

    b There were five people at the dinner table that night. .....

    c Sir Michael died in a locked room. .....

    d K arrives less than an hour after his death. .....

    e Sir Michael was poisoned. .....

    f His body was found behind his desk. .....

    g He drank a lot of whisky before he died. .....

    h K finds other people's fingerprints in the study. .....

After you read

4 Answer the questions. Who:

    a is a young detective?

    b will probably lose her job now?

    c called for help when she couldn't open the study door?

    d called the police?

    e take photographs of the body?

    f looks carefully at Sir Michael's shirt?

5 Discuss why these are important to the case.

   a the study door and window

   b the whisky glass

   c Sir Michael's shirt

   d the dictaphone

Pages 9–19

Before you read

  6 Imagine that you are K.

   a Which of these questions have you got answers to?

     Who? When? Where? Why? How?

     Are you happy with your answers?

   b What are you going to do next? Why?

While you read

  7 Write *believes*, *knows* or *doesn't know* in each sentence.

   a K .... that Sir Michael was killed with something sharp.

   b She .... that he wasn't poisoned.

   c She .... that he didn't kill himself.

   d She .... that the murderer was a man.

   e She .... how the murderer left the room.

   f She .... that he wasn't killed through the keyhole.

  8 Write one or two words in each sentence.

   a Sir Michael and his .... arrived at seven o'clock.

   b His wife, her .... and the Colonel were in the house.

   c They all spent time in the .... before dinner.

   d They ate in the dining room at .... o'clock.

  9 Write *says* or *doesn't say* in each sentence.

   a Mrs Flack .... that the Grays' guests were unhappy at dinner.

   b She .... that Sir Michael and Lady Elizabeth had a disagreement.

   c She .... that at 9.30 Sir Michael refused to open the door.

d She .... that Miss Everett wasn't with the others at that time.

e Lady Elizabeth .... that she loved her husband.

f She .... that her husband spent too much time with his secretaries.

g She .... that Angela Everett killed Sir Michael.

h She .... that she told her brother about her problems.

After you read

10 Work with another student. Have these conversations.

   a *Student A*:   You are K. Ask what happened this evening.
   Student B: You are Mrs Flack. Answer K's questions.

   b *Student A*:   You are Lady Elizabeth. Answer K's questions.
   Student B: You are K. Ask about Sir Michael's women friends.

Pages 20–34

Before you read

11 Discuss possible questions for K to ask Colonel Fawcett, Angela Everett and Andrew Cavell. Make notes on your ideas.

While you read

12 Underline the word in each sentence which is wrong. Write the correct word.

   a Colonel Fawcett drinks whisky with ice.   ....

   b He has known Sir Michael for thirty years.   ....

   c Sir Michael gave him a lot of money.   ....

   d Sir Michael was angry when Colonel
   Fawcett spent the money.   ....

   e The two men were soldiers in the army.   ....

   f Colonel Fawcett was alone in the
   dining-room at 9.30.   ....

   g Angela Everett says that she loved 'her Mike'.   ....

   h She will receive nothing from his will.   ....

i She and Sir Michael usually had a drink
together before dinner. ....
j Tonight Sir Michael was angry with her,
so she went upstairs. ....
k Andrew Cavell didn't like the way Sir
Michael spent the Gray family's money. ....
l He isn't happy that his sister's husband
is dead. ....
m He was with Lady Elizabeth in the
dining-room at 9.30. ....

After you read

13 Look back at your notes for Activity 11. Were you right about K's
questions?

14 Discuss the possible reasons that Colonel Fawcett, Angela Everett
and Andrew Cavell had for murdering Sir Michael.

Pages 35–44

Before you read

15 Discuss why K wants to talk to Mrs Flack. What does she want to
ask her this time?

While you read

16 Read pages 35–40 and write the names. Who:

a drinks, or drank, whisky with ice? ....
....
....

b read Sir Michael's letters? ....
c wanted Sir Michael's life to change? ....

17 Answer the questions on pages 41–42, and check your answers
on page 42. Then read pages 43–44 and write your guesses here.

Who? ....

Why? ....

How? ....

After you read

18 Work with another student and have this conversation.

> Student A: You are K's boss. You are at the police station. You want to know what is happening with the case. Telephone K and ask her questions.
>
> Student B: You are K. Answer your boss's questions.

Pages 45–59

Before you read

19 K knows how Sir Michael was murdered. Look at the picture on page 45. What is she doing? What do you think her answer is going to be?

While you read

20 Complete these sentences. Write one word in each sentence.

> **a** The freezer was at the same height as Sir Michael's ....
>
> **b** Sir Michael was killed by an ....
>
> **c** Sir Michael left .... to Angela Everett in his new will.
>
> **d** After everybody goes to bed, K waits in the ....
>
> **e** The .... is the next person into the room.
>
> **f** While he and K are talking, the murderer is ....
>
> **g** She planned to kill Sir Michael's ...., not Sir Michael.
>
> **h** By the morning after the crime, K has .... the case.

After you read

21 Discuss these questions.

> **a** Why was the use of an icicle a very clever idea?
>
> **b** Why didn't Mrs Flack's plan work?
>
> **c** Why can K feel happy about the result of her first case?

22 Work in groups of three and have this conversation.

> Student A: You are K, and you are talking to newspaper reporters after the case. Look at the pictures on page 46 and describe the last twenty-five minutes of Sir Michael's life. (You do not want to give much personal information about Sir Michael, his friends and family to reporters.)

Students B and C: You are newspaper reporters. Listen and ask questions. Find out as much information as you can about Sir Michael's life and death as you can.

Writing

23 Choose a picture from the book. Explain who and/or what it shows. What was happening at this point in the story? What did K know? What did she need to find out?

24 Write a newspaper report of Sir Michael's death. Who was he? Where, how and why did he die? What is going to happen now?

25 Is K going to be a good detective? Write her boss's report on her after her first case.

26 Explain why a big house is a good place for a murder story. What other places should writers of murder stories think about for similar reasons, in your opinion?

27 Imagine the future life of one of these people: Lady Elizabeth, Colonel Fawcett, Angela Everett or Andrew Cavell. How will his or her life change after Sir Michael's death? Will life be better or worse?

28 Imagine that you are Mrs Flack and you are now in prison. Write a letter to your sister. She is older than you and can't visit you. Tell her what happened in court. Explain how you feel now. When will you leave prison? What will you do after that?

29 Write about another murder story that you have enjoyed. What happened in the story? Why did you like it?

30 Write a short murder story. Use these words from the Word List at the back of the book in your new story:
case fingerprint inspector poison will

WORD LIST

army (n) all the soldiers that fight for a country

bow (n) a shaped piece of wood that you shoot pointed sticks from

carpet (n) a soft, heavy covering for a floor

case (n) a crime, or a number of crimes, that the police or a detective have to understand

colonel (n) an officer with a very important position in the army

dictaphone (n) a small recording machine that you speak into

engineer (n) someone who makes the plans for roads, bridges or machines

fingerprint (n) a sign that something was touched by a finger

gamble (v) to try to win money on the result of a horse race or a game of cards

housekeeper (n) a person who works in a house or hotel. A housekeeper often does the cooking and cleaning.

ice-tray (n) a flat tin in which you make square pieces of ice

icicle (n) a thin, pointed piece of ice that usually hangs down

inspector (n) a police officer

jealous (adj) feeling angry or unhappy. You want something that another person has.

loyal (adj) always ready to help a friend. Loyal friends never speak badly of you.

mechanism (n) a part of a machine that makes something work

poison (n) something, for example in food or drink, that can make you very ill. Strong poison can kill you.

string (n) something long and thin that you often buy in a ball. String is tied around boxes, for example.

whisky (n) a strong drink made, for example, in Scotland and Ireland

will (n) a paper that you prepare before your death. It says who will have your money after your death.